# Bitcoin

*21 Step Guide to Buying, Selling, and Mining Bitcoin*

© **Copyright 2017 by Roger Bray - All rights reserved.**

The following eBook is reproduced below with the goal of providing information that is as accurate and reliable as possible. Regardless, purchasing this eBook can be seen as consent to the fact that both the publisher and the author of this book are in no way experts on the topics discussed within and that any recommendations or suggestions that are made herein are for entertainment purposes only. Professionals should be consulted as needed prior to undertaking any of the action endorsed herein.

This declaration is deemed fair and valid by both the American Bar Association and the Committee of Publishers Association and is legally binding throughout the United States.

Furthermore, the transmission, duplication or reproduction of any of the following work including specific information will be considered an illegal act irrespective of if it is done electronically or in print. This extends to creating a secondary or tertiary copy of the work or a recorded copy and is only allowed with express written consent from the Publisher. All additional rights reserved.

The information in the following pages is broadly considered to be a truthful and accurate account of facts and as such any inattention, use or misuse of the information in question by the reader will render any resulting actions solely under their purview. There are no scenarios in which the publisher or the original author of this work can be in any fashion deemed liable for any hardship or damages that may befall them after undertaking information described herein.

Additionally, the information in the following pages is intended only for informational purposes and should thus be thought of as universal. As befitting its nature, it is presented without assurance regarding its prolonged validity or interim quality. Trademarks that are mentioned are done without written consent and can in no way be considered an endorsement from the trademark holder.

# Table of Contents

Introduction ............................................................................. 1

Chapter 1: Buying Bitcoin .......................................................... 3

Chapter 2: How to Sell Your Bitcoin ........................................ 21

Chapter 3: How to Mine Bitcoins ............................................. 36

Conclusion .............................................................................. 55

# Introduction

Congratulations on purchasing this book and thank you for doing so.

The following chapters will discuss some of the basics of getting started on the Bitcoin network. Many people are just now hearing about Bitcoin for the first time, and because of all the benefits, they have decided that it is time for them to join the network. But before you decide to join the network, you need to understand how it all works. This guidebook is going to take some time to talk about how Bitcoin works and how you can get the most out of your experience.

This guidebook is going to talk about a lot of different topics that come with the Bitcoin network. First, we are going to talk about how to purchase Bitcoin so that you can join the network and start doing the transactions that you would like. We will then move on to how to sell your Bitcoin. Whether you are looking to get out of the market and want to sell the rest of your coins or you would like to do this as a type of investment, learning how to properly sell your Bitcoin and the different channels that you can sell through can make the difference. And finally, this guidebook is going to end with some information on how you can choose to help the Bitcoin network, while still earning money, through the process of mining.

There is so much that comes with the Bitcoin network and learning how to get started with this network can help you to get in on some of the excitement. Take a look through this guidebook so that you can learn the best tips for buying, selling, and mining Bitcoin no matter what level you are at.

There are plenty of books on this subject on the market, thanks again for choosing this one! Every effort was made to ensure it is full of as much useful information as possible, please enjoy!

## Chapter 1: Buying Bitcoin

So you have decided that you are ready to join the Bitcoin network. You may have heard about this network for some time now and all of the benefits that come with the network. There are quite a few of them available, from being able to work on transactions without anyone being able to see who you are or any government interference. Some people like being able to use Bitcoin to invest and make some money. They may like how low the fees are, how much money they can save, and even the speed of finishing all of their transactions compared to traditional forms of banking.

Before you can jump into the Bitcoin network and start doing the trades and transactions that you want, you need to purchase some Bitcoin. You can use Bitcoin in any way that you like, whether you want to use them to make purchases, invest, or even to sell them later when the value goes up. But you need to go through and make the purchase first.

In this chapter, we are going to start with the basics of how you can purchase your Bitcoin and join the network. It is a pretty simple to join, but you need to take the right steps to avoid fees and to get it done as quickly as possible.

## Pick out the exchange site you want to use

When you are ready to purchase some Bitcoin, you need to pick out a good exchange site that you want to work with. There are a few that you can choose from, so how do you know that you are going with the right one? There are a few things that you will be able to choose from, but you do need to go through and come up with a good plan and think it through ahead of time. Some of the things that you should look for when choosing your exchange on the Bitcoin network includes:

- Liquidity: Because Bitcoin is in a market where the users are trying to sell or purchase the currency, it is important to realize how much liquidity the exchange has. Liquidity is basically the ability to sell your coins later on without the price changing a lot or a big price drop. The more sellers and buyers there are in the market, the more liquidity there is in a particular market. You can take a look at the different exchanges that you want to work with and see how high it is. For example, the mtgoxUSD exchange has a monthly volume of about 1.2 million while bitstampUSD has a volume that is about 260,000. This shows how liquid the market is with each one and can help you make your choices.

- Fees: When you decide to sell and buy Bitcoins, you are going to have to pay some money to make this happen. This is the main incentive for the exchanges to be run as a business and keep going. However, Bitcoin exchanges are a bit different than purchasing a stock or bond in that they will charge you a percentage. This means that the more you exchange in the Bitcoin network, the more you will be charged. If your 30-day volume is under $500, you will be charged a fee of 0.50 percent, but if you are going to trade up to $100,000 you could be charged 0.24 percent.

- Proximity: Bitcoin is still a currency that does not have a lot of regulations on it, but it is likely that this will start to change as more government intervention comes around. Many governments want to get involved to make sure that people are not avoiding taxes, doing illegal drug smuggling, terrorism, or even money laundering. Because of this future government regulation, it is important to know the location of your exchange before you choose to go with one. When you know where the exchange is, you will know what laws you have to work with while using that exchange. Often it is best to go with the one that is in your own country because you will already know most of the laws.

You can also take some time to look at some of the other features that come with Bitcoin and working with each exchange. You want to make sure that you are at least picking out one that meets the requirements that are listed above, but you also want to make sure that it is going to meet some of your own needs, that it has some good features, and maybe even find ones that have a few deals when it comes to the fees that you will pay. The right exchange is going to make a big difference in how much you enjoy working on this network and can help you to get some of your transactions done whenever you are ready!

**Set up your payment method**

One thing that you will need to consider before you get started with purchasing your Bitcoin is that you need to set up the right payment method. You have to be able to provide some payment method to change your traditional currency over to Bitcoin. Most exchanges will offer a few different methods to get this done, but you need to pick out the one that works the best for you.

The first option that you can work with is your bank account. You can transfer money directly from your account over to get the coins that you would like to use. This method works nicely if you would like to exchange larger amounts of your currency at one time so you will not have to worry as much about the limits. One thing to realize with this method, which is the major drawback, is that you have to wait three to five days before the funds can be available for you to use. If you want to be able to get your transactions started right away, this is probably not the best method for you.

You can also choose to work with PayPal or your credit card. These methods are going to be a lot faster, getting the transactions done in just a few minutes. This makes it the perfect choice if you would like to get your transactions started with Bitcoin right away. However, there are going to be some issues with the limits of money that you can transfer over at a time. If you want to be able to transfer larger amounts of money at a time, then using PayPal or your credit card may not be the best method.

You can choose to use whichever method that you would like. Your exchange is going to ask for a little bit of information to get this started, such as your bank account number and routing number or your credit card information. Once this information is in the system, you can choose how much currency you would like to switch over to get the exchange done.

And it is as simple as that. Remember that Bitcoin is all about the user experience so this company wants to make sure that you can have a great experience the whole time. Part of this is to make sure that a currency exchange between your traditional currency and the Bitcoin that you want is simple and easy and as you can see, this process can be done in just a matter of minutes in most cases.

**Watch the exchange rate for the best deal**

Before you get started with Bitcoin, you need to make sure that you understand how much you are going to need to spend. If you want to have ten Bitcoins, you need to see the exchange rate to figure out how much of your traditional currency you will need to come up with to end up with ten Bitcoin.

The exchange rate is going to change each day. The value of Bitcoin is going to go up and down each day, and you can check it all the time to see that the price is never the same. Right before you are ready to make the purchase, you will need to check out that exchange rate and make sure that you understand how much you will spend. Your costs will be different based on the type of currency you are exchanging from. For example, you will spend a different amount based on whether you are using the US dollar or the Euro.

In addition, you have to pay attention to the amount of fees that will be charged by the exchange rate to get the work done. Most exchange rates are going to charge you a little fee to help switch your traditional currency over to Bitcoin. Usually, this is not too much, but it is something to calculate into your costs.

**Pick out a wallet**

Once you choose the amount of coins that you would like to work with, you need to have some place to store the coins. This is going to be in the form of an online wallet to start with (although you can switch it over to cold storage as well if you would like), Picking out a wallet can be difficult. You need to find one that has the right features in play, and that will keep your coins secure no matter what. Some of the things that you should consider when picking out a Bitcoin wallet include:

- Decide what type of wallet: you can choose from an online wallet, a hardware wallet, or an offline wallet. The online wallet is often the easiest to use because all of your coins will be right there when you want to use them, but they are more susceptible to hacking. Hardware and offline wallets are better if you would like to store the coins for some time and you do not want the hackers to have a chance at them.

- How much security: when you are picking out a wallet, you will want to consider how much security that you would like to have. The amount of Bitcoins that you plan to store in the wallet will help you determine how much security you would like to have. More security that you go with, the better off your coins will be.

- What is your operating system: you also need to consider what kind of operating system that you are using when picking out your wallet. There are some wallets that will work no matter what operating system you are working with. On the other hand, there are some that will only be able to work with certain operating systems so you will have to look at their requirements before you pick one out.

- Services and features offered: there are different features that are available based on the type of wallet that you choose to use for Bitcoin. Bitcoin is about the user experience, and there are some wallets that will introduce some new features to ensure that their customers will stick around. This makes the market more competitive, so you have a lot of options. When you are picking out the wallets that you would like to work with, take some time to look at the different services and features that are available and figure out which ones are the most important to you.

- Ease of use: the type of wallet that you choose to go with will help determine the ease of use. There are a lot of the wallets that are available so it does not make sense to pick one that is hard to use or does not have the features that you would like.

Picking out a good Bitcoin wallet is one of the most important things that you can do. You want to make sure that you are picking out a good one. This is where you will store your coins when they are not in use, so you want to make sure that it has the best security and features possible so you can enjoy Bitcoin as much as possible.

## Pick out the Bitcoin address you are comfortable with

When you sign up for a Bitcoin address, you will get the choice to pick out your own Bitcoin address. This address is going to be like your username when you are on the network. Whether you are purchasing some new Bitcoin, selling your Bitcoin, making purchases, or mining the coins, you will need this address. This information will show up on your blockchain as soon as you are done with a transaction no matter what kind it is.

The idea of this address is to keep your information safe. You will be able to pick out whatever kind of address you would like to work with, but you should pick out one that does not give away your identity. One of the main reasons that people are going to choose to work with the Bitcoin network is because it allows them to stay hidden from others, making their transactions without others being able to see what you are up to.

There are a few things that you will be able to do to make sure that you are getting the right Bitcoin address. First, make sure that you do not use your name in the address. Nothing is easier for a hacker than to look through the addresses and see your name. They will then be able to link your transactions right back to your account, and they can then dig right in to your coins and use them how they would like.

You need to go with a name that is unique and all your own. It should really have nothing to do with your name, where you live, where you went to school, your spouse's name or anything else like that. It should be completely random so that it is harder for others to figure out who you are so you can keep things secure.

One thing to remember is that this security is going to disappear a bit when you are using the Coinbase wallet. This is a popular wallet that a lot of beginners choose to work with, but they will just use your full name to create the address. To keep with security, sign up for your own Bitcoin address and consider switching your coins from your Coinbase account over to another wallet so you can just rely on that new address.

## Options for buying your Bitcoin

There are actually quite a few methods that you can use when it comes to purchasing your Bitcoin. You can do it online, you can use a Bitcoin ATM, and you can even meet face to face with someone to complete the transaction. Often the choice that you make is going to depend on which one makes you the most comfortable. Let's take a look at how these all work so you can pick the option that is best for you.

The first option that we will look at is over the counter or face to face trade. If you want to avoid giving away your identity or you live in a city, one of the easiest ways to get the Bitcoin that you would like is to meet with the seller. LocalBitcoins is a great site to visit to arrange one of these in person transactions and to negotiate the price. It also provides an escrow service so that both parties will have some protection along the way.

While this method is pretty secure, you have to remember that there are a few things to consider in terms of security, especially if you are doing a larger trade. You should always meet in a busy place, rather than at someone's home and take precautions when you are carrying around a large amount of cash. It is also possible to visit the site Meetup.com so that you can go to a Bitcoin meetup to receive your coins. This method allows you to meet a lot of interested Bitcoin sellers and it is done in a safe and secure manner.

You can also choose to purchase your Bitcoin on a Bitcoin exchange. Sites like Coinbase work well in the United States, and you really only need to provide a little bit of information to get started as a buyer, such as your name and the Bitcoin address that you would like to use. You will also need to add in some kind of payment methods, such as your bank account, PayPal address, or a credit and debit card to start. From here, you can check what the current rate of exchange is and then get the coins that you would like to use.

An investment trust is one option that some buyers will go for. If you are not fond of the idea of having to purchase and then store large amounts of Bitcoin in a safe way, you can work with an investment trust. Two popular options with this include The Winklevoss ETF and the Bitcoin Investment Trust. The idea behind these is that you will be able to take your Bitcoins and store them safely without having to hold onto them for yourself. The fund right now is saved or really serious investors, but it is starting to add in some more people as time goes on.

Bitcoin ATMs are starting to become more popular as well, even though they are a pretty new concept and they are usually just available in a few places throughout the world. There are several vendors who are choosing to invest in these, so it will not be long before more are available. The Bitcoin ATM is going to work similar to a face to face exchange, but you will work with a machine. The ATM can scan your mobile wallet, or you can insert your case, and you will receive a receipt that will hold onto all the necessary codes so you can load the coins into your wallet.

If you are using one of the Bitcoin ATMs, you have to remember that the exchange rate can always change and that there will be a fee that is somewhere between three and eight percent above the standard exchange price for the convenience of using this machine. But if you are in a hurry to get the coins or you just like how easy it is to use these machines, the Bitcoin ATM can be the right choice for you.

**Pick out good sellers to work with**

When it comes to making some transactions on the Bitcoin network, you need to make sure that you pick out some good sellers to work with. There are a lot of different sellers on the marketplace, but not all of them are going to be the best for you to choose from. And when you send your coins over, you will find that it is impossible to send them back unless the seller agrees to reverse the payment.

The good news is that there are many reputable companies that are already working on the Bitcoin network. Some companies like Overstock.com and more have already decided to accept Bitcoin as a form of payment, just like they do with PayPal, credit card, and more online. These sellers already have a good reputation so it will not be too hard for you to get started working with them and you know that your purchases will be safe.

But the place you really need to be careful is in the Bitcoin marketplace. This is kind of like working with Craigslist, but you can work with Bitcoin instead. With this option, you have to behave just like you would when trying to make purchases with Craigslist. Vet all of the sellers that you want to work with, talk to them thoroughly about the product, and be careful before you send over any of the money for the products that you want.

There are some sellers who are going to have reviews on them, and these are often the safest for you to work with. You can go on various sites to find these reviews or the seller may provide them to you to show more trust in the system. Always take a look at these reviews if you would like to. These reviews can help you to figure out whether a seller is going to provide you with a good quality product that will get there on time or if the seller has some issues and you will never see your money again.

In addition to directly working with some of the sellers on the market, there are some methods that you can use to indirectly use your Bitcoin. We will talk about this a bit in the next section, but another option that you can use is to purchase Bitcoin. There are some big retailers and sellers who may not directly take Bitcoin at this time, but you can choose to purchase gift cards with your Bitcoin (there are a number of sites that will allow for you to do this) and then you can use those gift cards to make your purchases. It is not the most direct method available, but it does help you out.

The good news is that there are a lot of reputable sellers, both big companies, and individuals, who are joining this market. This means that you can find a lot of the products on this system, from all parts of the world, and make the purchases that you want with the help of Bitcoin. Whether you are just getting on the network to purchase something in particular or you are looking to stick with the market to make most of your purchases, there are a lot of great sellers that you can choose to work with.

Many people throughout the world are interested in choosing Bitcoin as the digital currency that they want to use. But to use this currency, you first need to purchase some. This chapter provided some of the steps that you need to take to ensure that you are properly purchasing the Bitcoin you need to get started.

## Chapter 2: How to Sell Your Bitcoin

There are some situations where you may decide that it is time to sell your Bitcoin. You may be done working on the network and want to get out of it, although most people who decide to sell their coins will do so to earn some money. They can hold onto the Bitcoin for a bit of time and then sell them when the price is higher, also adding on a little convenience fee to cover any costs that they would incur.

To get started with selling your Bitcoin, you need to be prepared for the work at hand. You not only have to already own some Bitcoin, but you need to be able to find the right exchange site, and the right buyer who will match the price that you want and this can take a little bit of time. But if you are dedicated to the work and know what steps to follow, you will be able to sell your Bitcoin and make a profit, in no time.

**Check the exchange rate for current prices**

Before you decide to go through and sell your Bitcoins, it is important to figure out how much these Bitcoins are worth.

It does not make sense to go onto an exchange or to try and sell the coins if you have no idea how much they are worth. You can easily sell them for too much, which means that no one is going to be interested in making the purchase. Or you could sell them for too low, which will get rid of them for you but which will make it hard for you to make a profit or get what they are worth.

The best place to look to figure out what you should charge when you are working with Bitcoin is one of the exchange sites. Coinbase is a good place to start, but there are a few others. This is going to give you a good idea of how much the coins are worth and what a fair price is to sell them. You do need to remember that there are going to be some fluctuations in different countries and if you choose to sell in a country that may be having some issues trading in Bitcoin, you could possibly ask a higher price for your coins for the convenience.

In addition to selling the coins based on the current exchange rate, most sellers are going to choose to add on a little bit of a fee to the price. This is to help them make a little bit of a profit from their work and is known as a convenience fee. Most buyers know that they will have to pay this fee so they will be fine with it. You can take a look on some of the exchange sites to see what other sellers are adding as a fee to help you stay competitive when it is time to sell.

Checking the exchange rate is going to help you to know the costs of doing business. Not only will it give you an idea of how much you will have to spend to get the value of Bitcoin that you would like, but you will get a good idea of the amount that the exchanges are going to end up charging you. There are some costs for exchanging in the Bitcoin network and making the purchases, so be careful and make sure you know all of them upfront.

## Selling through direct trades

The first thing that you should consider for trading your Bitcoin is to do it through a direct trade. There are a few different websites that offer this structure, so you have some options. In the United States, you would use LocalBitcoins or Coinbase, but there are also a few other options based on where you live in the world.

When using the direct trading sites, you will need to start by registering yourself as a seller. This will involve you providing some proof of your identity. Once you are registered on the site, you can post your offer, which indicates to the site that you want to sell your coins and then the website will send you an alert when there is a buyer who wants to trade with you. After the website alerts you of this buyer, you will move all transactions over with the buyer, but you would use the website to complete the trade and keep everything safe.

Coinbase and LocalBitcoins keep their exchanges pretty simple. As long as you provide the information that is legally required for them to prove who you are as a seller, you are set to go. You can pick out the price that you want to work on with the buyer and then complete the transaction when you are ready. Some of the exchanges that are available in other countries will be more involved, and you will have to give them some patience so be aware of that if you are not exchanging in the United States.

**Selling through exchange trades**

Some people decide to sell their Bitcoins through an online exchange. This one is going to require that you verify your identity, but it is not quite as intensive as what you would need to do when organizing the sale. The exchange site is going to act as the intermediary in that it will hold onto everyone's funds until the exchange is done. You would start by placing a sell order, similar to how you would place a buy order. This should state the volume and the type of currency you are looking to sell, and the price that you would like to sell it for.

Now, someone on the other side of things is going to place a buy order that will say how much of the Bitcoin they would like and how much they would like to pay. When there is an order that is matching, the exchange will go through and complete this transaction. The currency is then going to be credited back to your account.

While these exchanges are going to be pretty easy for you to use, there is a downside. If you are working to sell your Bitcoin for traditional local currency, you will need to remove that currency from your wallet over to your bank. If the exchange is having issues with liquidity or there are issues with its banks, it can take some time before you get your funds out.

You can also choose to use a pure cryptocurrency exchange. What this means is that you would trade out your Bitcoin for some other digital currency. There are not as many people who would like to work with this one, but sometimes it is a good idea if Bitcoin goes down in value and the other currency goes up because it can save you a bit of your investment.

One thing that you have to keep in mind is that you will probably have to pay some kind of fee to work with these exchanges. Each exchange will charge you a different amount to use them. For the BTC-e exchange, you will receive a fee of 0.2 percent no matter how much you exchange. It is a good idea to check on the fees that you will be charged before you decide to use the exchange.

Another thing to consider is that there will be some limits to the money that you can store on the exchange and this amount is liable to change over time. No matter what this change becomes, it is not a good idea to use these exchanges to store all of your coins, although some beginners feel that this is the best and easiest way to go about things. In reality, this is just a form of speculation and can be completely risky. You need to take responsibility for the funds that you have and store any amounts that you do not need offline or somewhere else so that you do not need to worry about hackers.

## Selling through peer-to-peer trading marketplaces

A new development that is being used in the Bitcoin network is known as peer to peer trading. This is when some sites like Purse and Brawker are going to bring together two parties who have specific needs that will complement each other.

The first group is going to be individuals who would like to be able to use their Bitcoins to purchase goods from some sites that do not accept these digital currencies. While Bitcoin and the other digital currencies are growing in popularity, there are still a lot of major retailers who are not comfortable with accepting these currencies as a form of payment. The first type of peer to peer trading would allow the user to do this by paying someone else with Bitcoins and then that second person will use their traditional currency to purchase the items for the other person and can keep the Bitcoin.

The second group is going to be others who would like to purchase in to the Bitcoin network using their debit card or credit card. They would use some of their traditional currency to pay someone else to purchase Bitcoin for them so that they could use the digital currency how they would like. The idea of the marketplace is to bring together these individuals who have matching requirements so that they can sell their Bitcoins and provide discounted goods to others.

The marketplace is going to be the intermediary that makes all of this happen because it will offer the escrow, the Bitcoin wallet, and the platform that the users will need to use. The way that these works are as follows.

- Person one is going to post their Amazon wish list on the marketplace, stating the discount you are looking for, which will usually be somewhere under 25 percent.

- Person two has a debit or a credit card, and they want to purchase Bitcoin that will match the value of Alice's purchases. Person two is going to accept the trade, and through the help of the marketplace they will purchase the Amazon goods and sends them to person one.

- Once person one receives the goods, they will notify the marketplace, and then person two's Bitcoin will be released from escrow and be placed in the wallet. There will be a little bit taken out based on the agreed discount and the small fee to pay the marketplace.

This system is a little unfair to the second person because it means that they will usually have to pay a pretty high service fee for the exchange. But the benefit of doing this means that the second person will be able to get the Bitcoin that they want just from using their debit card.

## Understanding the rules of identity verification for sellers

This is a part that a lot of beginners have some trouble with. They are used to being able to go on the Bitcoin network, purchase their coins, and make the purchases that they want without having to give away too much of their personal identification. This is one of the biggest benefits that comes with using the Bitcoin network. But when you are trying to sell your Bitcoin, there will be a little bit of identity verification for you to go through as the seller.

Most of the Bitcoin markets that you will choose to work with will require very little in terms of verification for the buyer. But as the seller, you will need to prove who you are. There are very few legal requirements for these Bitcoin markets to record who the users are, but most are starting to collect some of this identity data because they feel that some regulations are going to come in the future. This will definitely change the way that Bitcoin is traded in the future.

To make it easier to become a seller on this network, it is a good idea to consider doing the whole process for identity verification when you first join your site. This may be a bit of a hassle, but it will remove some of the barriers to becoming a seller whenever you decide that it is time to make a move.

When you decide to go through identity verification, you will need to upload a few things. This could include a photo ID which would include your driver's license and your passport as well as two utility bills that include your address and your name. There are some of these sites that could ask you to take a selfie and will want the photo ID as well. Make sure to take a look at the site that you plan to use to determine what you need to add into it.

If you do not feel that comfortable uploading these personal documents to a business like this, you could run into some trouble later on. It will help to save you some time and some barriers later on when you are ready to sell your Bitcoins online.

## Selling coins locally

Another option that you can try out is to sell your Bitcoins locally to someone in your area. Of course, you need to make sure that you can find this person, but with the popularity of Bitcoin growing so quickly, it is becoming more likely that you will be able to work with. Selling your Bitcoin in person is often the easiest way to pass on the currency, so if you can find someone in your area who would like to have them, it can save you a lot of time and hassle. You often just need to scan the QR code over to another person's phone and then accept the cash payment for it and then you are done.

If you know someone who would like to purchase the Bitcoin, the process is simple as long as you make sure to meet up with them in the right place. They will need to have a Bitcoin wallet in place so that you can send over your coins to them, but other than that, you do not need to have much. However, there are a few things that you should be cautious about when it comes to selling Bitcoin.

First, you and the buyer need to decide on the price that you would like to work with. A good place to start is to decide on a price by looking at the Bitcoin exchange or the Bitcoin Price Index. This helps to show what the going rate for these coins is at the time of sale. In addition, it is not uncommon for a seller to add on a small percentage on top of these rates to cover some of their costs of transferring things over.

As you are deciding on the price that you want to use, it is good to be aware of the local fluctuations that occur. Prices will and can vary from one country to another, and sometimes this is due to how easy or difficult it is to obtain more Bitcoin with the national currency of that area. This can sometimes affect how much the coins are going to be worth in your area.

As a local trader, it should not be too difficult for you to find people who would like to purchase your coins. In some cities around the world, there are even some Bitcoin meetups. During these, you will be able to meet with others who would like to trade their Bitcoins and even some other digital currencies, so you will be in good hands there.

When you are deciding to sell your Bitcoin locally, and there is quite a bit of cash involved, it is a good idea to bring along a friend or two to be safe. You can recommend this for your buyer as well so that neither of you run any risks while meeting up. Pick a place to meet that is well-lit and in a popular location so that others would see if something weird was going on.

If you want to sell locally but you do not know a friend or family member who would like to purchase the Bitcoin, you can also advertise to a bigger audience with options like LocalBitcoins. This kind of website is going to allow users to put a rating on each other so you can see how trustworthy you would be as a trade partner. You can work on getting a reliable reputation and then sell with a premium compared to some of the other sellers. This site also does not ask you to verify your identity, so this can help you to remain anonymous.

**If you sell your coins locally, meet in a safe place**

There are many times when you will decide that you want to sell your Bitcoins locally. This method is often one of the easiest, and you will not have to worry about sharing your identity online like you do with some of the other options. However, it is important that you stay safe when you are going to meet someone to do the exchange. It is hard to tell who is talking on the other side when you work with a buyer, and you will want to make sure that you are staying as safe as possible.

The first thing to remember is that you need to pick a safe place to meet. Never meet at night in an alleyway or something like that. This makes it easy for the other person to screw you over or even attack you, taking your Bitcoins without ever paying you in the first place. The best thing to do is pick out a place that is out in the open, where a lot of other people will be around, and meet up during the day. A local grocery store or a popular restaurant can be good places that will ensure that both you and the buyer are safe.

Many times it is a good idea to bring a friend along when you want to sell your Bitcoin. It is nice to have someone else there to look things over with you and to make sure that you do not get harmed in the process. You most likely do not need this person around all that much, but it can be nice to have them there to protect you in case the buyer you are working with is not that trustworthy. Do not be surprised if the other person brings someone along as well. They have never really gotten a chance to know you except for maybe online (unless you are trading with a friend or family member) so it could be in their best interest as well.

If you talk to this person online before you meet up, make sure to ask some questions and have a few conversations before you meet. Many times you will be able to catch on to the ones who have bad intentions early on and can stop the transaction before you meet up. Most f the people that you meet on these sites will be fine, but it is always better to be safe than sorry with people you are dealing with online.

Selling your Bitcoin can be a bit of a process to deal with. You need to be able to find a buyer who would like to take the Bitcoin for a price that you are comfortable with, you need to find a way to transfer the money over to you, and a way to send your coins over to the other person. But if you follow these tips, you will b able to find the perfect method for selling your Bitcoin in no time.

# Chapter 3: How to Mine Bitcoins

One thing that has started to gain a lot of popularity in the Bitcoin world is the idea of mining. Mining is basically the process of generating more coins that can be used by the rest of the Bitcoin network. Bitcoin was designed to only have 21 million coins, but not all of these coins were released at the same time. The miners can come into the mix, and when they are done with their work, they will release a few more coins.

Mining can be hard work, and not everyone can complete that work. It requires the user to be able to solve some complex algorithms and to keep things organized. A good strong computer with the right software can make all the difference as well. Let's take a look at some of the tips that you can follow to see some success when it comes to mining Bitcoins.

## Understanding the rules of Bitcoin mining

As a beginner, it is important that you understand some of the rules that come with mining Bitcoin. These rules are in place to make sure that the hashes you are creating will work out for the blockchain and that the information stays safe.

A quick review: The Bitcoin network is a way to make payments and receive money without needing to have a third party or an intermediary there to handle the payments. This helps to lower the transaction fees and will ensure that the transactions are done in just a few minutes. However, there needs to be an element of trust in the whole thing, or no one is going to use the network in the first place.

The work of the miners is to make sure that the blockchain stays safe. Once they receive a new part of the blockchain, they will work to create hashes that will keep the information secure. But as competition grows for doing this work, the algorithms will get tougher and more and more people will try to do this work.

If you want to be paid for your work as a miner, you need to make sure that you are following the right rules. For example, each number that is in your hash needs to be reliant on the number or character before it. So if one number in the chains is changed, this is going to change all the numbers that come after it. This can make it hard to work with, but that is the point. It allows others to see if a hacker tried to get in and mess with the system.

Bitcoin also requires that there are so many zeroes that are put in front of the hash as well. The miners can add in some information to help create the hash that they need, but they cannot modify, remove, or change the information that is already there, or they will be in trouble.

Creating one of these hashes can be difficult, which is why there are so many people who will work on them and why the reward is so high. But if you stick with it, and even if you decide to work with a mining pool, you will find that it can be a good return on investment.

## Consider a mining pool

There are a few choices that you can make when it comes to mining Bitcoin. Some people decide to jump into the whole thing and do the work on their own. This can be really hard. You need to have a good computer, a great power source, and the ability to solve some pretty complex algorithms without the help of anyone else. Because there is so much competition that comes with mining these Bitcoins (because there is such a good profit that comes from it). It is possible to do the work on your own, and it will yield some good profits in the process, but the competition is so fierce that you may find that your success rates are low.

This is why some people decide to work with a mining pool. With a mining pool, you and some other miners will come together to work on these complex algorithms. Instead of having to do all the work on your own, you can split up the work and the power with others who want to mine. You will have to split the profits, but at least you have a better chance of earning something without having to do all the work.

When you decide to work in one of these pools, you are going to get to work on just part of the algorithm rather than working on it all on your own. You will be sent the algorithms that you should work on and then there will be some other people who are using the same pool who will solve other parts of the algorithm. Then all of the work can be combined to make it easier for everyone to get it done rather than having to do the work on your own.

Once all of the work is done, all the people in the pool who did the work will share the reward, with the coins being split up based on how much of the algorithm you ended up solving. While you may not be able to earn the whole reward with this option, you will earn something, and it is a much better return on investment compared to trying to do the work on your own. You will consistently earn coins this way, rather than hoping that you can compete on your own against everyone else.

Of course, you do need to take some precautions when picking out the mining pool that you will join. There are several pools that are available for you to use, so you can look around and see which one will provide you with the best options. For example, some pools offer a larger amount of money, some will offer you more work and so on. Some of the questions that you need to have answered before you join in with a mining pool include:

- What does their reward method look like? Are you able to figure out how much you would make for the work that you do, or can you figure out how the money is split up?
- When you decide it is time to take your funds out, are there any fees that you have to take and how much are these?

- Is there consistent work with this mining pool? If the mining pool does not have a lot of work, you are not going to make all that much money in the process.

- Is it pretty easy to use these mining pools and then take the funds out later when you want?

- Has this pool been around for some time or are they having some trouble remaining stable?

It is important to remember that you should ask these questions before you decide to join a new network. They will help you to understand what you will get paid and if this is the right option for you. Since you are looking for a mining pool without Bitcoin, go ahead and check out BitcoinTalk. This website has some threads about this topic, and you can go to the Bitcoin page to see the different comparisons between the mining pools that you are considering. Once you have a good idea on which mining pool may be the best for you, you can go ahead and get started.

Finding the mining pool that you want to work with can be the hardest part. Each pool is going to have some requirements in place to make sure that you are going to really help them. They do not want to hire someone who does not work hard and who could cost everyone else a lot of money in the process. You also have to worry about finding the right mining pool, the one that will provide you with the best price for your work and which will actually send you a payment when the work is done.

There are still some people who choose to do the mining process on their own because they like to earn the whole reward on their own. But as the process for Bitcoin mining becomes more complex and harder to keep up with, it is going to be harder for these individuals to do the work on their own as well. Because of this, most successful miners are going to join in with a mining pool and will choose to do the work along with others and take their part of the payment.

**Go for powerful and updated hardware**

Before you decide to get started with mining Bitcoin, you should choose what kind of hardware you would like to work with. There are not a ton of hardware requirements that you need to follow, but having a strong computer with all the right parts can make it easier to mine your Bitcoins and get the results that you would like.

When Bitcoin was first developed, it was possible for the miners to just bring out their regular computer and then they could get the mining down. The process was pretty simple, they just needed to solve some mathematical equations, and at the time, they were able to use the regular CPU that was on their computer. So anyone who belonged to the network was able to get the mining work done as they needed.

However, the difficulty for mining on the Bitcoin network has gotten much harder, mostly because there is a lot more competition that has been thrown into the mix. It is pretty near impossible to use your regular CPU to mine. Instead, users will need to work with some extra power on their computer to accomplish their goal and using a GPU can make things easier.

Now it is more of a competition to successfully finish mining, and most miners are trying to produce and use computers that has more power behind it. Most miners who are successful will choose to use powerful graphics cards to do the work for them. If you want to create a mining machine or you are interested in purchasing one, you do need to make sure that it has enough GPU's on it. These are strong and will demand a lot of power behind them, so you need to have a good power source as well. To be successful, you have to make sure that you have enough power so that your system will stay stable while the work is done.

So, we have just talked about needing some more graphics to start, but what else is needed in terms of the hardware on your system. You will first need to have a more advanced computer that has as many graphics cards as you can manage to help do the work. There are some miners who are ambitious and will choose to create their own mining machines, but even if you do decide to purchase one, it needs to have as many graphics cards as possible. These graphics are doing to help you to compete against the other miners, so you can actually earn some money in the process.

You will also need to make sure that you also have the basic motherboard in addition to having as many of these graphics cards as you can. You will also need to have a good hard drive to hold onto all of this information, although most miners will not choose to store their mined coins on the hard drive for safety reasons. Once these are in place, you can get started with the software that is needed to help with mining.

**Choose the right software**

Choosing the right software to help set up your mining operating can be so important. You already have the right hardware to make sure that your computer can handle all of the work that you want to do, but now you also have to make sure that the right kind of software is in place as well. The software that you decide to use will need to solve the complex mathematical equations that you are sending through to earn the coins. You can try to do this all on your own, but in most cases, you will find that it is much easier and more efficient to choose some software to do the work.

Since you will have worked on your mining rig all from scratch at this point, you will need to go through and make sure that you have a good and strong operating system in place. It is common for personal computers to use Windows operating system because it can handle a lot of different processes on your computer. However, this is not the best operating system to work with when you want to mine in

Bitcoin. In fact, some people who have been mining in Bitcoin for a long time will suggest that you do not use the Windows operating system because it is not the most trustworthy here and could pose some security risks.

If you are looking to install a new operating system to use in your endeavors, you should consider going with the Linux operating system. There are actually a few versions of Linux that are optimized for the mining process, such as BAMT and LinuxCoin. The second one is only able to work with the LiteCoin option, but you can use them to help you get your mining done.

The Bitcoin page does have some other mining software options that you can use, and you can pick out the options that you would like to use based on whether you plan to use the Linux, Mac, or Windows operating systems. When you get there, you will notice that this Bitcoin page is set up kind of like a Wikipedia page, with lots of good information that you can use to learn more about Bitcoin if you would like.

Once you know the operating system that you want to work with and all of your chosen mining programs are installed, it is time to pick out which wallet you would like to use to store your Bitcoin when you are done. As you go through the process of mining the Bitcoin, you have to have a place where you can store these coins safely, and the wallet will be able to help you to do this. There are a few different types of wallets that you can work with, you just need to take a look at some of the features that you want to use and then pick the wallet that goes the best with those.

When you pick out a wallet and start putting some coins inside of the wallet, you will receive a private key. This key is going to consist of a long list of letters and numbers, and it is meant to keep your coins separate from the other wallets that are on the network. You can store this key wherever you would like, printing it off, storing it on your online wallet, or even on the hard drive of your computer. Make sure that you store the key somewhere that you can easily access it but is still hard for others for others to get ahold of.

At this point, you should have all of your software in place, and the hardware on your computer should be all set up. The biggest obstacles of getting started with this mining process are done. You can jump into mining process, deciding to either jump in and do all of the work on their own or choosing to work with a mining pool to get the work done. No matter what method you choose at this point, it is time to start mining!

**Install a Bitcoin miner**

One thing that you may want to consider doing is setting up a Bitcoin miner. This is basically going to be the software that you can use that will tell the hardware how to behave. You do not want to go through and do all of the work on your own. These algorithms can be really complex, and they can take a lot of time to complete on your own, taking you out of the competition for others who have the right software that can do the work for you.

The bitcoin mining software is going to be the part that will instruct the hardware to do the work for you while also passing through all of the transaction blocks that you need it to solve. There are quite a few that you can work with, but your choices will be limited based on what kind of operating system that you are using. There are miners that are available for Linux, Mac, and Windows systems.

You may decide that you need some of this mining software for your ASIC miner as well. There are a few newer models of these miners that will promise to send everything over to you at once, including the Bitcoin address that you can use. This can be nice for some beginners because all they need to do is plug the system into the wall and then they can get started. Others prefer to do this all on their own so that they can ensure that their information is safe and secure.

## The benefits of cold storage to keep your coins safe

When it comes to storing your Bitcoin after you successfully mine them, you probably already know that you need to place them into a wallet. There are a lot of different wallets that you can pick from and often it will depend on how you would like to use them and the features that come with the different ones that you are looking to use.

While wallets are good places to store the coins if you plan on using them pretty soon, there can be some problems when you would like to store the coins for some time. Some miners like to keep the coins there so that they can increase in value over time and others just do not want to pay the fees with exchanging them all the time, so they wait until a certain threshold is met. But the longer that the coins stay in your wallet, the more susceptible they will be to a hacker or a computer glitch taking them all.

This is why it is recommended that you switch to cold storage for your coins. Cold storage basically means that you take your coins off your online wallet and store them somewhere else for safekeeping. You would basically do this with a special key that tells the network how many coins should be there. So even if something happens with your online wallet, you still have all of the information that you need.

There are a few different types of cold storage that you can work with and often it is recommended that you use a few different options to make sure that your coins stay safe. The first option is to store your key on your hard drive. This one can be susceptible to hacks if someone can gain physical access to your computer, but overall it is safer than working with an online wallet. Plus, you get the benefit of being able to easily access the key without having to take a lot of extra steps.

Some people choose to move the key over to a storage device that is not on their hard drive. This could include something like a USB drive. You can copy the key over to the USB drive and then store it in some place that is safe and easy to find later. Make sure that the USB drive is somewhere that you will be able to find easily but is secure from other sources. If you end up losing that USB drive, you could end up losing all of your coins.

Another option is to choose to print off the key to your coins. You can print off the unique code, that will include numbers and letters, and then store it in a safe place. Since it is on a piece of paper, this is something that can be pretty easy to lose. Store it in a safety deposit box or somewhere that you know it will not get lost so you can access your code whenever you would like.

You also need to remember that you should back things up on a regular basis when you are working with these coins. Each time that you use the coins, or each time that you successfully mine some more coins, go and make another backup of your key. Any changes to the coins need to be recorded on your key. If you try to use a key that has not been updated, you will get the old results; it is not going to automatically update your cold storage for you.

**Put on a good antivirus to stop hackers**

If you are mining Bitcoin, you need to make sure that you have a good antivirus and a good malware in place. You are potentially going to store a lot of Bitcoin online or on the hard drive of your computer, and this means that a lot of hackers are going to want to try and get the information.

Many beginners will pick out a wallet to use online and will store their Bitcoins in there as they go. Often they will have that wallet hold the Bitcoin for some time, waiting until they can get to spending the Bitcoin, waiting for the value to go up more so they have more money, or just waiting to reach a certain threshold before they do an exchange. Either way, it is common for miners to leave their coins in their wallets for some amount of time.

This can spell out bad news, especially for those who have quite a few coins and who haven't done the right steps to make sure that their coins are safe. If a hacker can get onto the wallet that you are using, by hacking into the database, they could potentially take all of your coins. Even if you store your coins on your hard drive, the hacker has the potential to go through and wipe all of the coins out of your wallet.

The biggest issue here is that once the coins are gone, you will not be able to get them back. There is no big entity that you can go complain to any group that will be able to help you restore the coins that you have. Once the coins are gone out of your wallet, you are stuck without anything. And wouldn't it be a big shame to lose out on all of those coins because you didn't have the right kind of antivirus in place to take care of yourself?

Always make sure that you have a good type of antivirus and a good malware in place before you join any of these networks and start mining. You also need to be careful that you are not clicking on any links, either in your email or online, so that you can make sure your information stays safe. In addition, stick with some of the cold storage options that we described above so you can ensure that your coins will stay safe for you to use whenever you would like.

Mining in Bitcoin and other cryptocurrencies can be a lot of fun. There is a unique challenge that comes with working on this project, and the reward can be great. But you do need to make sure that you are following the right steps and getting things done in the right way. When you are ready to get started with mining, make sure that you check out this chapter and learn the best tips to make sure that this happens.

# Conclusion

Thank for making it through to the end of this book, I hope it was informative and able to provide you with all of the tools you need to achieve your goals in buying, selling and mining Bitcoin.

The next step is to get started on the Bitcoin network. Bitcoin is probably one of the best known digital currencies that is out there, and because of this, there are thousands of people all over the world who are interested in learning more about this great way to send, spend, and earn money. This guidebook went over some of the basic steps that you need to know to join the Bitcoin network, make purchases, and even how to mine through the Bitcoin network.

The process of purchasing Bitcoin is pretty easy to work with, but you need to understand how to set up your wallet and how to work with the exchange of your choice so you can turn your traditional currency over to Bitcoin. Chapter two taught you about selling your Bitcoin. If you have decided to invest the Bitcoin and wanted to sell them or you want to get out of the market for some reason, it is best to refer back to chapter two to walk you through some of the steps that are needed to sell those Bitcoin. In addition, the final chapter looked at the simple steps for mining Bitcoin and some of the things that you will need to make this easier.

Working with the Bitcoin network can be really fun and exciting for a lot of people, but it does take a few steps to make sure that you get it all set up. Make sure to read through this guidebook to refer back to all of the tips that you need to begin just like a professional.

Finally, if you found this book useful in any way, a review on Amazon is always appreciated!

www.ingramcontent.com/pod-product-compliance
Lightning Source LLC
Chambersburg PA
CBHW050021230526
45470CB00003B/1074